OFF TO CHHATTISGARH

SONIA MEHTA

PUFFIN BOOKS

An imprint of Penguin Random House

PUFFIN BOOKS

USA | Canada | UK | Ireland | Australia | New Zealand | India | South Africa | China | Singapore

Puffin Books is part of the Penguin Random House group of companies whose addresses can be found at global.penguinrandomhouse.com

Published by Penguin Random House India Pvt. Ltd
4th Floor, Capital Tower 1, MG Road,
Gurugram 122 002, Haryana, India

Penguin
Random House
India

First published in Puffin Books by Penguin Random House India 2018

Picture Credits

ISBN 9780143440888

Design and layout by Quadrum Solutions Pvt. Ltd

Printed at Repro India Limited

Hello Kids!

I'm so happy you are reading this book. India is an incredible country and there are lots of things about it that we never get to hear about.

I discovered India because my father was in the Indian army. He was posted to many places all over India—and we dutifully followed him. Can you imagine that by the time I was in the tenth standard, I had changed nine schools? Of course it was hard making new friends almost every year, but the good part was that I got to live in so many places. Right from Kerala, where I was born, to Kashmir, Jhansi, Shillong, Chandigarh, Goa . . . the list is long.

Every time I go to a new place, I feel amazed at how different each state is from the other—and yet, how similar. Did you know that we can see monuments from the Stone Age right here in India? Or that we have more than twenty official languages, and most Indians know three or four on an average? Or even that some of the world's most amazing scientific marvels were invented in India?

Oh, there are many, many, many fun and fantastic things about the states of India, which we simply must get to know.

So get your backpack ready, get set to meet some new friends and join me on a fun trip as we DISCOVER INDIA, STATE BY STATE.

I hope you enjoy reading this book as much as I have enjoyed writing it. I would love to hear from you. So do write to me at sonia.mehta@quadrumltd.com.

Lots of love,
Sonia Aunty

Mishki and Pushka have come to visit Earth from their home planet, Zoomba. They have never seen such an amazing place. Zoomba doesn't have trees and mountains and rivers like Earth does. But the people look exactly the same. When they come to Earth, they meet a sweet old man whom they call Daadu Dolma. Daadu Dolma shows them all the wonderful places in India and tells Mishki and Pushka all about them.

Mishki and Pushka can't believe what they see. They have seen a lot of Earth, but they have never, ever seen a place like India.

They are off to explore India state by state :)

Mishki

Mishki is a curious little girl. She is always asking loads of questions. On her home planet, she is always getting into trouble for poking her nose into things that are not her business.

Pushka is Mishki's brother. He loves adventure. He is always ready for a new challenge. Whether it's climbing a mountain, or diving into a cold, cold sea, he is up for it.

Daadu Dolma

Daadu Dolma is a wise old man who has lived on Earth longer than the mountains and the seas. No one knows quite how old he is, but he certainly has been around. He knows everything about everything.

Pushka has woken up extra early. He shakes Mishki, who is still fast asleep.

'Wake up, sleepy head!' Pushka yells into her ear. 'We have to leave soon.'

Daadu Dolma comes in to see if the children are ready. Mishki wakes up with a start. 'Are we going already? I wanted to ask you so much about Chhattisgarh before we leave,' she says.

'Well, you can ask me on the way. Chhattisgarh is a small state, but there's a lot to see,' replies Daadu. 'So hurry up!'

Mishki and Pushka get ready at top speed. They are beyond excited because they are

OFF TO CHHATTISGARH!!!

A SNEAK PEEK

LAND AHOY!
About the land, water, rivers, mountains and seas.
page 6

LONG, LONG AGO
The story of the state.
page 14

TALK TIME
What language do the people speak?
page 20

BRICKS AND STONES
Of houses, buildings and bridges.
page 30

A PEEP INTO THEIR LIFE
The music, dance and lifestyle of the people.
page 22

STANDING STRONG
Famous monuments in Chhattisgarh.
page 32

WORKING HARD
What work do people do?
page 40

YUM YUM YUM
Food, food, food. What's the yummy food of Chhattisgarh?
page 44

AUTOGRAPH, PLEASE?
Famous people—past and present.
page 50

WHAT TO WEAR?
The clothes they wear.
page 48

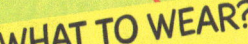

ONCE UPON A TIME . . .
Stories from the state.
page 54

Land ahoy!

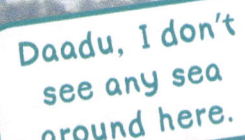

Daadu, I don't see any sea around here.

That's because Chhattisgarh is surrounded by land on all sides. A bit of it has some lovely rivers and waterfalls that you will enjoy visiting.

ON THE MAP

To see exactly where Chhattisgarh is on the map of India, go to

http://www.mapsofindia.com/maps/india/india-political-map.htm

FRIENDLY NEIGHBOURHOOD

Chhattisgarh has some friendly neighbours on all sides. It is surrounded by Uttar Pradesh, Jharkhand, Odisha, Telangana, Maharashtra and Madhya Pradesh. Did you know that until recently this lovely state was a part of Madhya Pradesh? We'll later see how it became a state in its own right.

UPS AND DOWNS

A large part of Chhattisgarh is flattish. It sits in the basin of the Mahanadi River. But all of the state isn't flat. Thanks to years of being eroded by wind and rain, the land has knolls, gentle valleys, strips of clayey soil and interfluves (the land that is between rivers or water bodies).

Interfluves. I just learnt a new word!

The Mahanadi River

HILLS AND PLAINS

The massive Chhattisgarh plain is surrounded by different landforms. Here are the main landforms that circle it:

- Chota Nagpur Plateau
- Maikal Range to the west
- Hills of Raigarh
- Raipur Upland
- Bastar Plateau

RIVER RUSH

Chhattisgarh has some important rivers. Chief among these is the Mahanadi. This river has a long journey before it empties itself into the Bay of Bengal after passing through Odisha. Along the way, it meets other rivers, like the Shivnath. The Indravati, the Arpa and the Pairi are some of the other rivers that water this state.

The beautiful Indravati River

CROP HOP

Considering that so much of Chhattisgarh consists of plains, farming is really important. In fact, almost half of Chhattisgarh is covered with farmland. Many things grow here: rice, maize, millet, sugarcane, cotton and oilseeds.

Did you know?

Chhattisgarh grows so much rice that it is called the rice bowl of India.

What an amazing green the rice fields are!

COLOURFUL SOIL

Of all the different types of soil found in Chhattisgarh, two types predominate—black clay-like soil and reddish-yellow soil. The soil is rich in minerals. Iron ore, coal, tin, manganese, gold, copper and even diamonds are found in this soil!

WEATHER VANE

Chhattisgarh has three proper seasons—summer, winter and the monsoon. It gets super hot during summer, with dry, scorching winds. Winters are just right, and people enjoy the not-too-cold weather. And it thunders and showers during the heavy monsoon, something farmers eagerly wait for.

RANGE TRICK

Pushka is confused. He wants to describe a mountain range. Can you help him by circling the words that best describe a mountain range?

SNOWY   SLOPE   PEAK   SQUARE

ROUND   STEEP   SANDY   FLAT

FOREST FANTASY

Chhattisgarh has a pretty good forest cover, with trees like teak, sal, salai and bamboo. Teak is especially valuable, and there is an entire industry thriving around it. People make good use of bamboo as well, using it for many different things.

WILD AND WONDERFUL

You'll get to see lots of animals in the forests and reserves of Chhattisgarh. There are tigers, striped hyenas, black buck, spotted deer, sloth bears and four-horned antelope among others. Like in many other states, it has become important to protect these animals, many of which are endangered. There are several wildlife sanctuaries here, where animals can roam freely.

I'm waiting to spot some wildlife!

FUN FACTS

State animal
Wild buffalo

State tree
Sal

State bird
Hill myna

NATURE WORD SEARCH

The animals and trees of Chhattisgarh are hidden in this grid.
Can you help Mishki find them?

TEAK   SAL   SALAI   BAMBOO   TIGER   HYENA   BLACK BUCK   SPOTTED DEER

D	F	D	T	E	A	K	B	V	B	A
T	I	G	E	R	Y	U	H	E	R	Q
Q	W	E	R	G	G	H	A	S	I	W
S	D	S	A	L	A	I	X	Z	K	E
B	L	A	C	K	B	U	C	K	J	R
Z	M	N	B	V	C	S	A	L	Y	T
F	H	T	V	W	Q	J	A	B	H	G
S	P	O	T	T	E	D	D	E	E	R
X	F	H	Y	E	N	A	D	E	W	Q
Z	B	A	M	B	O	O	C	F	G	J
X	C	V	B	N	M	Z	X	C	N	K
Z	T	N	W	E	O	O	P	Z	X	V

CITY CITY BANG BANG

RAIPUR

Raipur is Chhattisgarh's capital and also its largest city. It's a busy place, with many industries sprouting up here. It's also an important historical city and is full of fascinating monuments and ruins.

A sculpture dedicated to tribal art in Raipur

BILASPUR

Another super busy city, Bilaspur is an important railway hub. Guess what it's most famous for? Its rice! A variety of rice called *dubraj* rice is well known, and people buy it by the kilo.

AMBIKAPUR

One of Chhattisgarh's larger cities, Ambikapur has an interesting history. It used to be the capital of a princely state. It got its name from Goddess Ambika, whom people worship fervently.

JAGDALPUR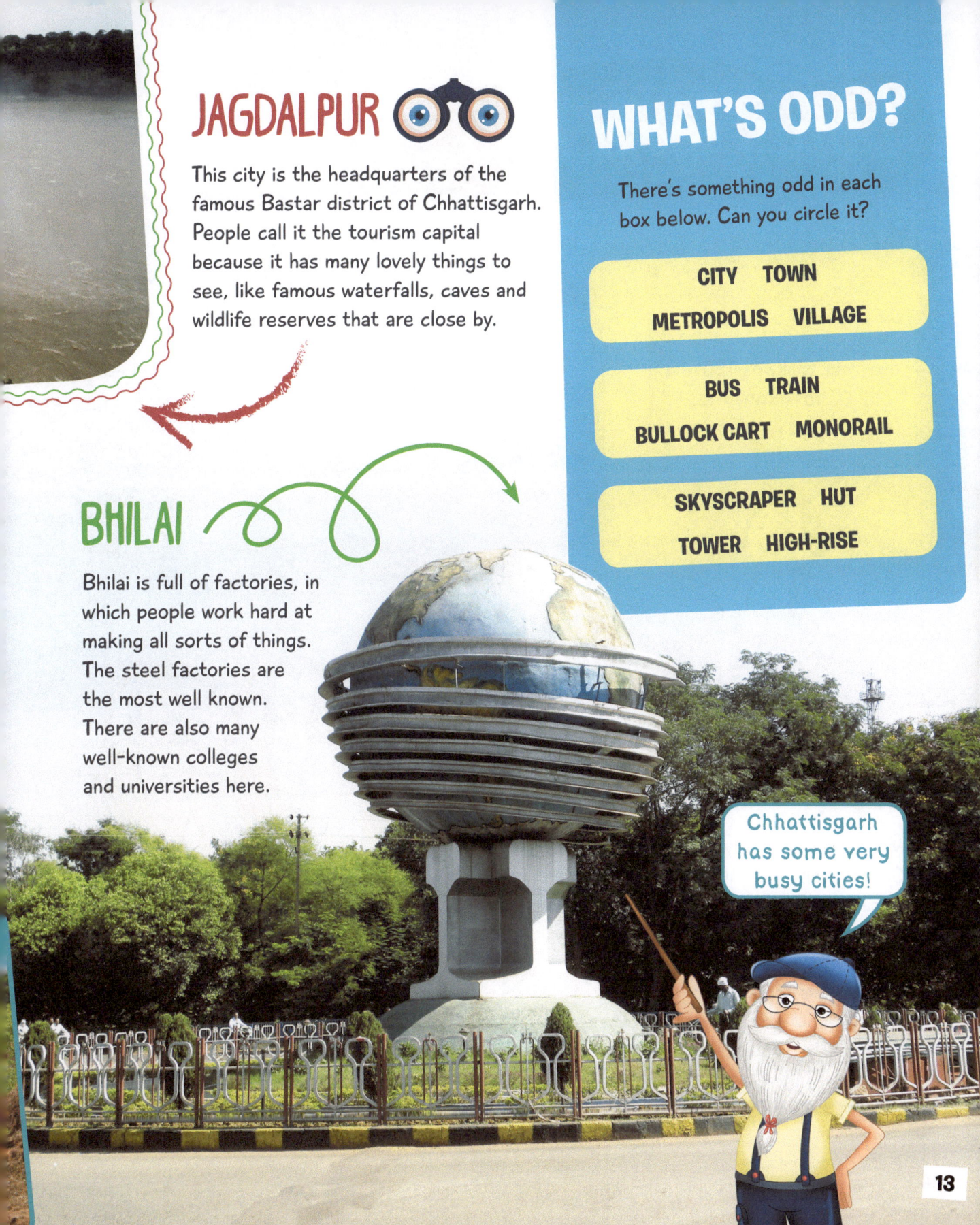

This city is the headquarters of the famous Bastar district of Chhattisgarh. People call it the tourism capital because it has many lovely things to see, like famous waterfalls, caves and wildlife reserves that are close by.

BHILAI

Bhilai is full of factories, in which people work hard at making all sorts of things. The steel factories are the most well known. There are also many well-known colleges and universities here.

WHAT'S ODD?

There's something odd in each box below. Can you circle it?

CITY   TOWN
METROPOLIS   VILLAGE

BUS   TRAIN
BULLOCK CART   MONORAIL

SKYSCRAPER   HUT
TOWER   HIGH-RISE

Chhattisgarh has some very busy cities!

Long, long ago

Daadu, I am really curious to know how old Chhattisgarh is. Does it have a long history?

Well, as a state, Chhattisgarh is rather new. But as a region, it has a long and interesting history with kings, wars and lots of excitement.

OLDER THAN HISTORY

Many thousands of years ago, Chhattisgarh was called Dakshina Kosala. Though there is not much documented evidence, scriptures suggest that Lord Rama spent a few years in this state while he was in exile with his wife, Sita, and brother Laxman. That's how old the state's history is.

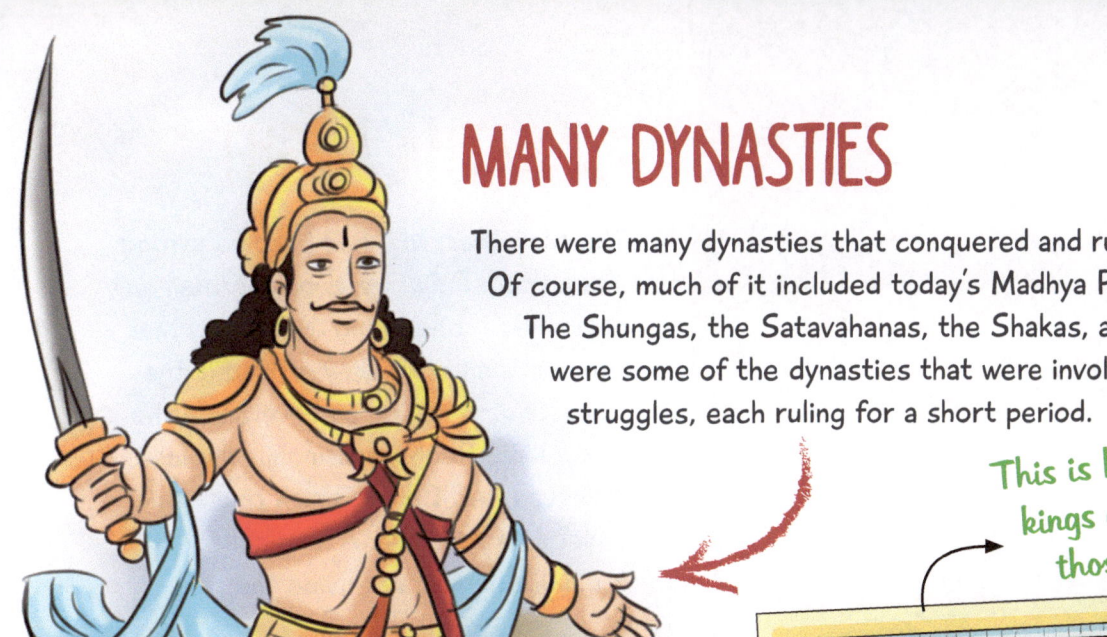

MANY DYNASTIES

There were many dynasties that conquered and ruled this region. Of course, much of it included today's Madhya Pradesh as well. The Shungas, the Satavahanas, the Shakas, and the Nagas were some of the dynasties that were involved in power struggles, each ruling for a short period.

A Satavahana king

This is how Rajput kings dressed in those days.

UNDER THE GUPTA EMPIRE

For a long time, the Guptas, who occupied a large part of northern India, ruled the region of Chhattisgarh and Madhya Pradesh. There were some fierce battles during this period, especially when the Guptas fought off the nomadic Hunas (also known as the Huns).

Coins tell us a lot about the past.

RULE OF THE RAJPUTS

One dynasty that ruled this region for a long time was a Rajput dynasty called the Haihayas. Historians believe that this dynasty ruled for over six centuries before it broke up when it was defeated by the Marathas.

MARATHA MIGHT

The Marathas, who had become strong in southern India, were making their way northward, conquering everything that came in their way. They arrived in the Chhattisgarh region and overcame the ruling king, Raghunathsinghji, the last Haihaya ruler. Chhattisgarh thus came under Maratha rule. A king called Bimbaji Bhonsle was made the ruler.

Maratha warriors were a strong lot.

There used to be fierce battles in those days. Warriors would fight head-to-head with swords and shields.

CHAOS AND CONFUSION

After Bimbaji Bhonsle died, the Maratha rule in this region became quite chaotic. Many soldiers broke away and went on a rampage. An outlaw group, the Pindaris, was creating havoc by harassing and robbing people. The region became weak and ripe for any invader to take over.

THE BRITISH RULE

By this time the British had identified India as the perfect place to colonize. They found it easy to overthrow the Marathas and take over Chhattisgarh. They made their own laws, which were often harsh on the local people. The people of Chhattisgarh rebelled, particularly the Gond tribe; they refused to accept British rule and fought hard against them.

SAME OR DIFFERENT

This Maratha warrior looks like he means business. Can you spot ten differences between the two images?

A TRIBAL REVOLUTION

Many tribes struggled and fought hard to keep the British at bay. The tribal people of a region in Chhattisgarh called Bastar started the Halba revolution. The Muria tribe in particular played an important role. This was a long and effective revolt.

Veer Narayan Singh was a local hero who fought valiantly and gave his life for the freedom of India.

These different tribes seem to have been a strong group.

SAVING THEIR TREES AND THEIR INDEPENDENCE

The tribals of Chhattisgarh embarked on many sustained revolts that showed how important their land and their independence were to them. The Koi revolt was a fierce protest against certain British laws that demanded the cutting of sal trees. The Koi tribe decided that they would not allow a single tree to be felled. They held fast against the British, who were forced to take a step back.

A FIGHTING SPIRIT

Many other tribes took to the streets, protesting the treatment of Indians, and tribals in particular. The Muria rebellion, the Paralkot rebellion, the Rani revolt, the Tarapur rebellion—these were just a few that demonstrated the fighting spirit of the people of Chhattisgarh.

INDEPENDENCE AT LAST

Finally, after the entire country rose and protested in a single united voice, the British were forced to go home and give India its independence. As we saw, the freedom fighters of Chhattisgarh played an important role in Independence.

THE BIRTH OF CHHATTISGARH

When India became independent in 1947, Chhattisgarh did not exist as a state. It was part of Madhya Pradesh. The people of this state always had a strong identity and were proud of their culture and roots. Well before Independence, they had demanded that Chhattisgarh be made a separate state. It was only in the year 2000 that Chhattisgarh became a state in its own right, with its own culture, history and identity.

Talk time

Wow! The tribes of Chhattisgarh seem to be really strong and proud. What language is spoken here? Can we learn a little?

Yes, absolutely. It's wonderful to know as many languages as possible. Come, let's find out what most of the people speak and also learn some phrases.

Did you know?
Chhattisgarhi is called different things by different tribes. Khaltahi, Laria and Dakshin Kosali are some.

The main language most people speak here is Chhattisgarhi. It is very similar to Hindi. But, of course, with so many tribes around, there are many dialects too. Let's learn some of the more common phrases in Chhattisgarhi.

You = Tain
Come = Aa
What? = Ka?

Where did you come from? = Tain kati le aaye has?

Your = Tor
What should I do? = Main kaa karon?
Yes, of course! = Haaho!

What is your name? = Tor naam kaa haawaye?

Is it a book? = Te kitaab hawaye ka?

How are you? = Tain kaise has?
I am fine. = Main bane ho.

MATCH THE WORDS

Daadu is testing how much Pushka remembers. How much do you recall? Match the English phrases to their Chhattisgarhi translations.

What?   Where did you come from?   Yes, of course   You   Your   What is your name?

Tain kati le aaye has?   Tor naam kaa haawaye?   Tor   Tain   Haaho   Ka?

A peep into their life

Tribal people of the Bastar region

Daadu, I've been observing the people here. Many of them seem to be members of tribes. Is that right?

In a way you are right. The tribes here give this state its true identity. Of course, there are many other communities too. Come, let's meet some people and learn about their culture.

TRIBAL TRACTS

It is said that many of India's oldest tribes are from Chhattisgarh. And some of these are more than 10,000 years old, especially those from the Bastar region of Chhattisgarh. The various tribes have their own beliefs and culture, but many have imbibed aspects of Hinduism.

TRIBAL MEET AND GREET

Let's meet some of the main tribes of this region.

The Gonds   The Abhuj Maria   The Bhatra   The Muria
The Halba   The Kol   The Munda

Though these tribes are different in many ways, almost all of them love and worship nature: trees, animals, the sun and the moon. Much of their music and dance revolves around nature.

The Muria tribe

A CULTURE OF CREATIVITY

Many tribal communities are famous for their unique handicrafts. Woodcarving, bell-metal and terracotta work, tribal jewellery, painting and dyeing—all these skills are available in plenty and are unique to Chhattisgarh.

Bastar art of Chhattisgarh

WORD JUMBLE

Mishki and Pushka want to remember the names of the tribes. But the letters are jumbled up. Can you help unjumble them to find the tribal names?

NGOD _____   BHAAL _____

HATARB _____   LOK _____

RUMAI _____   DUMNA _____

FOLKSY TUNES

There's a lot of music in the plains of Chhattisgarh. The various tribes have their own styles of music, and so do other communities. Chhattisgarh's folk songs are enchanting. There are many types, each with its own unique lilt.

CHAIT PARAH

This is a style of song that is sung during the changing of seasons.

PANDAVANI

This style of singing is in a story form, in which the singer narrates tales from the Mahabharata. It is a kind of folk theatre and one of Chhattisgarh's most famous.

LEJA

These are songs that are sung during farewell rituals, when loved ones leave and go away.

DADARIA

These songs are sung by the Kamar tribe. Also known as *ban-bhajans* or *salho*, the songs have a delightful rhyming pattern.

Did you know?
India's first university dedicated to music was founded in Chhattisgarh.

BHARTHARI

A royal saint called Raja Bharthari is the subject of these popular songs.

DHANKUL

People sing this in devotion to Goddess Danteshwari.

SING SONG

Mishki has decided to write her own song—that's how inspired she is by the tribal music of Chhattisgarh. Can you help her complete the song by adding the rhyming words? Her song is about the sun!

The sun is bright, it keeps us warm

It shines all through the day

It helps to keep us nice and dry

At school and at _____

The sun gives all of us energy

It helps the plants to grow

It warms the farms and rivers too

We need it, don't you _____?

But when it gets oh-so hot

We need to keep so cool

We sit under the shade of a tree

Or jump into a _____

Farmers love the sun so much

To grow all their crops

So that we can buy the grains

In our nearest grocery _____

THE CHANCE TO DANCE

Dancing is a popular form of entertainment among the tribes of Chhattisgarh. They love dancing, and there are many styles involving different skills.

SAILA

This is a group dance usually performed by men. It often takes place after the crop has been successfully cut. The dance is performed by striking sticks together to a beat. It's great fun to watch.

SUWA

This is also called the parrot dance. Tribes perform this to please the goddess of wealth. A parrot sitting in a bamboo pot is at the centre of the excitement, around which the dance is performed. There's another interesting angle to this dance. If a boy sees a girl whom he's interested in doing this dance, he can send a marriage proposal to her parents.

KARMA

This is a religious dance. The dancers lock arms and move in a circle. A branch from the karma tree, which is very sacred, is passed from one person to the next. But careful! The branch must not touch the ground. At the end of the dance, the branch is washed in milk and then planted.

RAWAT NACHA

This is as much a dance contest as it is an art form. Teams from different villages take part. A child is dressed as Lord Krishna, and each team sings and dances to the music of drums and flutes. The dance symbolizes the battle between the young Lord Krishna and his cowherd friends, and the evil King Kansa.

Looks like great fun! I am going to try these dances out.

DANCE DELIGHT

There are so many kinds of dances in the world. Can you circle them? There are ten dances hidden here.

Waltz

Jogging

Karate

Kung-fu

Samba

Kathakali

Ballet

Garba

Bharatanatyam

Dandiya Raas

Swimming

Bhangra

Cycling

Cha cha cha

Skating

Jive

Sleeping

GONCHA

This is one of Chhattisgarh's most popular festivals. People shoot bullets made of fruit from bamboo pistols. They aim and shoot at each other—all in the spirit of fun.

KAJARI

Farmers celebrate this to mark the beginning of the sowing season. They seek the blessings of Goddess Bhagwati. Women collect pots of soil from the fields and sow barley in them. They make lovely patterns on the ground with rice flour. They then carry the soil from the fields and immerse it in a lake or a pond.

This temple is ready for Dussehra.

BASTAR DUSSEHRA

Dussehra is one of Chhattisgarh's most important festivals. Dussehra celebrated in Bastar is known across India. It goes on for ten whole days. Hundreds of priests come from all over the state to the temples of Danteshwari Devi. There are songs, prayers, food and lots of fun too!

PHAGUN MADAI

It's time to celebrate spring. Every March, just before the festival of Holi, people begin to celebrate. They perform songs and dances based on local folklore. It's fun and full of music and colour. People come from across India to be a part of this fun festival.

Priests walking towards the Danteshwari temple

SHADOW MATCH

This man is all dressed up for a festival. Can you spot his shadow?

A   B   C

Bricks and stones

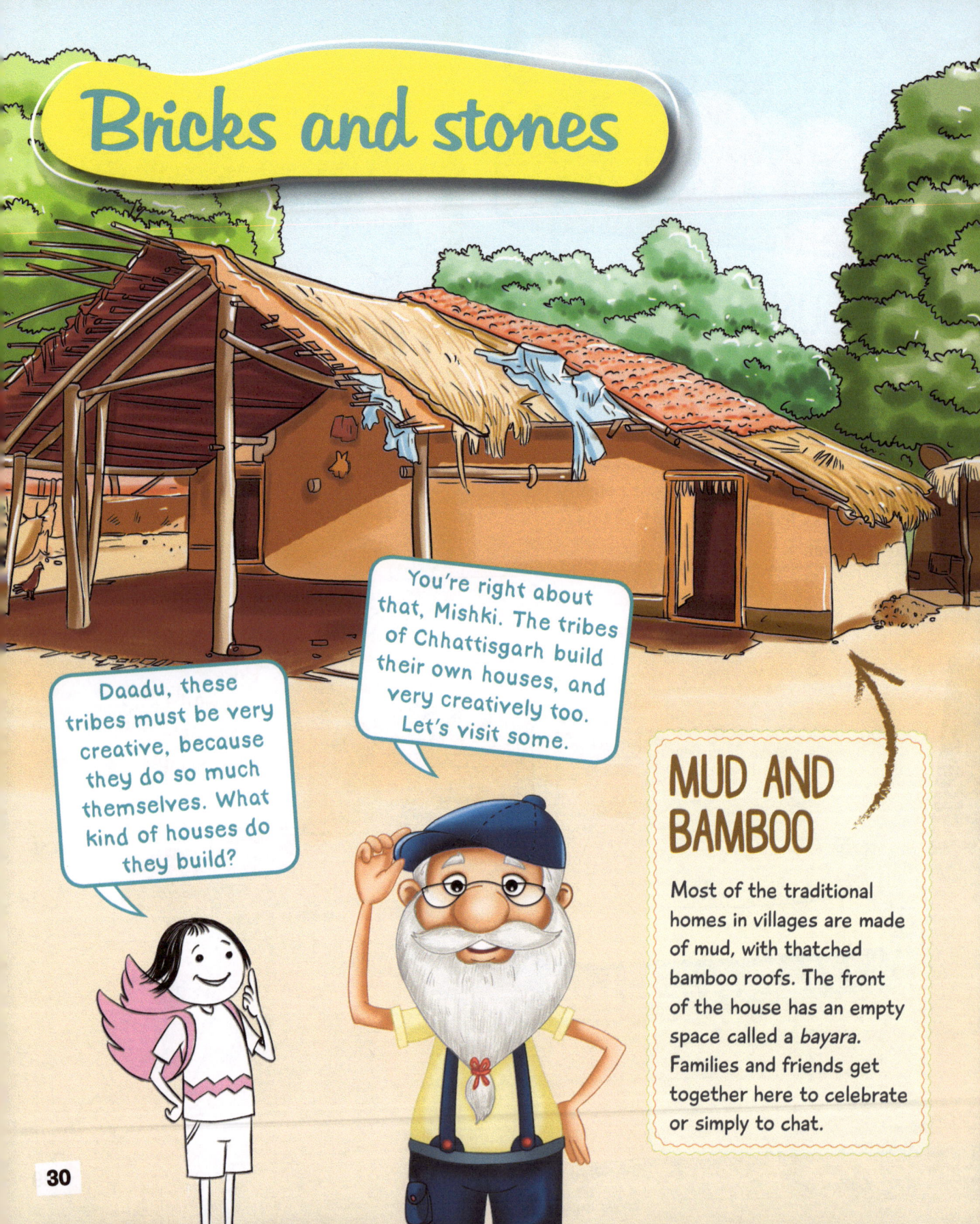

You're right about that, Mishki. The tribes of Chhattisgarh build their own houses, and very creatively too. Let's visit some.

Daadu, these tribes must be very creative, because they do so much themselves. What kind of houses do they build?

MUD AND BAMBOO

Most of the traditional homes in villages are made of mud, with thatched bamboo roofs. The front of the house has an empty space called a *bayara*. Families and friends get together here to celebrate or simply to chat.

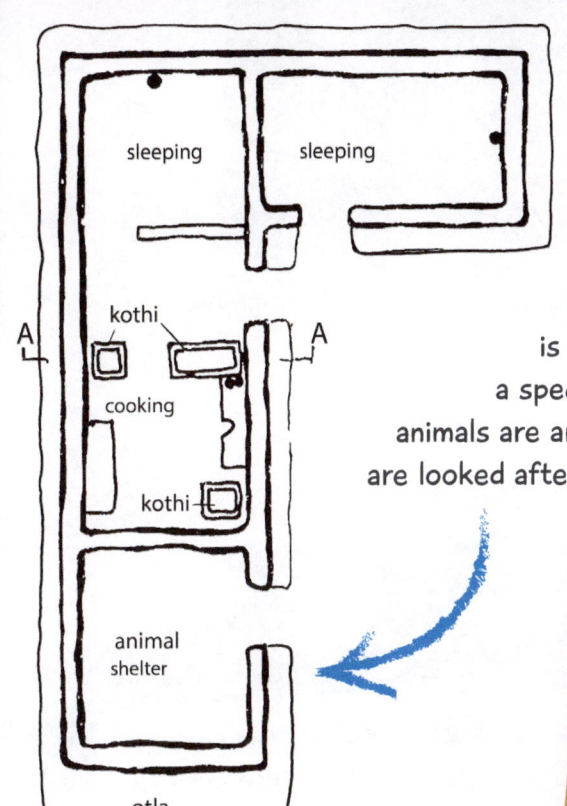

sleeping

sleeping

A

kothi

cooking

kothi

A

animal
shelter

otla

NICELY PLANNED

The side walls of the many tribal dwellings have a small platform called an *otla*. This is perfect to sit on and have a nice chat with neighbours and friends. The *kothi* is the place where people store their grains. There's even a special room for their animals. Isn't that considerate? Well, animals are an important part of their lives, so they make sure they are looked after well.

Otla

NO WINDOWS?

Most tribal houses here have no windows at all. That's because the thick walls keep the house cool during scorching summers. Instead, the house is ventilated by little slits in the roof. Of course, when it rains, the roof needs to be covered quickly.

The way houses are built tells us a lot about how people live. People who study the life and lifestyles of different cultures are called sociologists.

GOING MODERN

Now, with modern trends catching on, more permanent houses are being built, using cement, steel and bricks. In fact in the towns and larger cities, there are urban buildings like any other metropolis has.

Standing strong

Wow, Daadu. Everything looks so interesting. I wish I had lived all those years ago.

Well, if you want to feel like you're in the past, you simply have to visit some of the monuments and structures built so many years ago.

FABULOUS FORTS

Some say that the name Chhattisgarh, meaning 'thirty-six forts', came from the fact that there must have been many, many forts here.

LAFAGARH FORT

Lafagarh Fort, also known as Chaiturgarh Fort, is believed to be one of India's strongest natural forts. It sits majestically on the highest peak of the Maikal Hills. There are lovely carvings on the pillars and gateways. There is even a temple inside the fort.

RATANPUR FORT

This was once an impressive fort that is now tragically in ruins. But you can imagine how magnificent it must have been when you see what remains of the pillars and walls. Some exquisite stone sculptures of Lord Ganesha, Lord Shiva doing a dance, and Ganga and Yamuna (human depictions of the rivers) have survived to this day.

KOSAGAIGARH FORT

This fort has an exciting aura. It is camouflaged by thick forest cover, and the only way to get to it is through a secret tunnel. During battles, soldiers would hide in the fort and send rocks rolling down the hillside to stop unsuspecting enemies, who had no idea that an entire fort was hidden among the trees.

Stone carvings outside Kosagaigarh Fort.

MALHAR FORT

Here's an ancient fort that takes you back in time. Like a lot of really old monuments, this one too is in ruins. Some inscriptions that were found here were so old that they were moved to museums, where they would be preserved. The town of Malhar became very important during the reign of the Kalchuri dynasty.

TEMPLE BELLS

The temples of Chhattisgarh attract devotees and pilgrims from all over India, and even the world.

THE TEMPLES OF DONGARGARH

The deity that people pray to the most in this temple town is Maa Bamleshwari, a goddess that people have tremendous faith in. The main temple is dedicated to Badi Maa Bamleshwari. There's a smaller one that houses the idol of Choti Maa Bamleshwari. There are fairs and festivals that take place here, where thousands of devotees come to pray.

BHORAMDEO TEMPLE

This temple is called the Khajuraho of Chhattisgarh by some. This ancient Shiva temple has intricate carvings that remind visitors of the Khajuraho temples in Madhya Pradesh and the Sun Temple in Odisha. What skill and talent people had in those days!

BARSUR TEMPLES

Historians say that at one time, there were nearly 150 temples and ponds here. The temples, which are now over 1000 years old, are in ruins. There are many beautiful carvings of Vishnu, Shiva and Nandi (Shiva's mount). But the most popular is the Ganesha temple. Amazingly, two massive sandstone sculptures of Ganesha are still intact and stand proud.

SHIVRINARAYAN TEMPLE

This really ancient temple was built by a king from the Haihaya dynasty. This has mythological importance too, because it is here that Rama stopped to rest during his exile—or so legend goes—and it was here that a simple tribal woman called Shabari gave him berries to eat, only after tasting them first to ensure they were safe.

> What a pity that many temples are now in ruins!

CURIOUS CAVES

There are many caves in Chhattisgarh that are really very old. Let's peep into some of them.

SOME OF THE OLDEST IN THE WORLD

Singhanpur is most popular for its ancient caves. Some archaeologists say that the paintings found in these caves are among the oldest on earth, having been made in 3000 BCE. They look similar to ancient paintings found in Mexico and Spain.

The caves are also home to a rare species of blind fish.

PITCH BLACK OOOH! SCARY!

When you enter the Kutumsar Caves, you can truly understand what pitch black means! The caves are deep underground and have the most amazing stalactites and stalagmites. They are full of rich minerals. There are even natural chambers and some wells too!

Did you know?

Stalactites and stalagmites take years and years to form. It is said that it could take as long as 6000 years for an inch to form, because they form drop by drop.

OLDER THAN OLD

The Dandak Caves in Kanger are millions of years old. These also have spectacular stalactites and stalagmites. Some of them have strange markings on them. People believe that in ancient times devotees must have worshipped these.

CAVE MAZE

Mishki, Pushka and Daadu Dolma are lost in this cave, deep underground. Someone has thrown them three ropes. Can you tell which rope will get them out?

MONUMENT SPOTTING

There are many monuments on these pages. Can you spot the different monuments and places of interest from Chhattisgarh? Circle each one.

Working hard

Daadu, with so many tribes in Chhattisgarh, what kind of work do people do?

Well, tribes have lived off the land as farmers or goatherds for a long time. But now there are factories and businesses, and people work in different industries. Let's find out more.

RICE STORIES

As you already know, Chhattisgarh is also called India's rice bowl. Farmers grow lots of rice. There are many rice mills, where rice is polished and packed, and then sold all over India.

FARMER, FARMER, WHAT ELSE DO YOU GROW?

Rice isn't the only thing grown here. Maize, millet, cotton, oilseeds—these are just some of the other crops that giver farmers their livelihood. Many farmers also grow a leaf called tendu, which is used to make many things.

COWS AND SHEEP

Many tribal communities were goatherds. Now animal husbandry (the breeding of cattle and sheep) has become a rather important industry. Many, many people work in this business.

MINING AWAY

Because Chhattisgarh is so rich in minerals, there are many mines here. Coal, iron ore, dolomite and other minerals are found deep in the ground. There are lots of people working hard to get these minerals out of the ground and put them to use in factories, turning them into products we can use every day.

POWER TO POWER

Chhattisgarh produces a lot of electricity and even supplies it to other states. There are engineers who work in power plants, where electricity is produced. There are some dams too, where hydroelectric energy is created.

Dams are important because they help channelize river water so that electricity can be drawn from it.

A visit to a dam is very interesting.

SMART STEEL

Manufacturing steel is one of Chhattisgarh's most important industries. There are many, many large and small manufacturers who make different types of products from steel, like rods, steel plates and rails. All these are then used to build bridges, buildings, cars and many other things.

Oh, the people here are busy, all right!

FACTORY FEVER

Apart from factories that process minerals, there are many others that make different things, like cement factories and mills making sugar, paper, textiles and oil.

Sugar factory

Metal casting called dhokra is a famous handicraft in Chhattisgarh.

HANDY HANDICRAFT

There are some super skilled craftspeople in Chhattisgarh, who make the most wonderful things. There are potters who create artistic pottery; there are weavers who weave magical textiles and carpets; and there are others who embroider exquisite patterns using gold and silver thread.

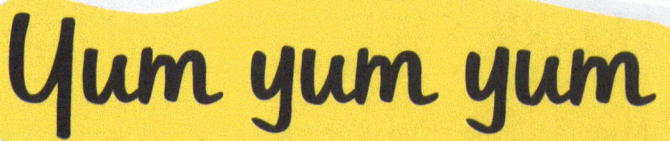
Yum yum yum

Well, you'll stop being hungry soon because we're going to taste some yummy food. Let's discover what food people in Chhattisgarh cook and eat.

Daadu, I'm very hungry.

RICE IS NICE

Chhattisgarh grows so much rice that many of its tastiest dishes are made using it. In fact, you could say that rice is Chhattisgarh's staple food.

BORE BAASI

This is a comfort food made from leftover rice. The previous day's rice is soaked overnight and eaten the next day along with pickles, tomato chutney, onions and chillies. It's supposed to be cooling too, so people have it during the hot summers.

MMMMM MAHUA

Some of the tribes here make a delicious drink from the small creamy-white fruit of a local tree called the mahua. This drink is famous across the state.

FARA FUN

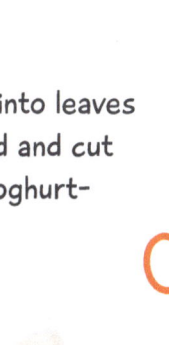

Here are some tribal momos. These dumplings are made of rice flour that is steamed. It's a tasty and healthy snack, perfect to have any time of the day.

INTERESTING IDHAR

This yummy dish is made by rolling ground dal into leaves called *kochai patta*. Layers of this are steamed and cut into small pieces. Then this is popped into a yoghurt-based gravy.

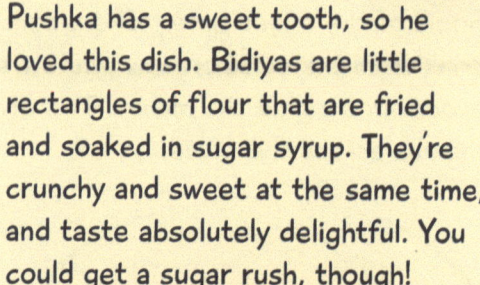

Pushka has a sweet tooth, so he loved this dish. Bidiyas are little rectangles of flour that are fried and soaked in sugar syrup. They're crunchy and sweet at the same time, and taste absolutely delightful. You could get a sugar rush, though!

BARA BITES

Whenever there is a fair or a festival, the one dish you are most likely to eat is bara. This is a bit like the famous vada from South India. It's a mixture of vegetables, lentils and spices that's turned into dumplings, then flattened and finally fried. Yummm!

BAFAURI BOOM

This dumpling is a cousin of the ever-popular pakoda, which everyone across India simply adores. The only difference is that instead of being fried, it's steamed, making it not just tasty but healthy too!

Looks delicious!

MUTHIA MAGIC

Many states make this dish called muthia—but the one cooked in Chhattisgarh is different. These are delicious boiled momos made of rice batter. It's a hugely popular dish with farmers, because it doesn't spoil easily and can be carried to the fields and eaten as a nutritious meal.

PERFECT PETHA

This sweet dish is a hot favourite of the locals. It's made by cooking pumpkin and then dunking it into a sugar syrup. It just melts in your mouth. Other states lay claim to this dish too, but Raipur boasts of some of the best petha ever.

RAKHIYA BADI

These are small beads made from a fruit called the *rakhiya*. The fruit is washed and left overnight under a stone. Then it is mashed, dried and turned into little balls. These are then popped into a curry. They can also be stored for later use.

Food Puzzle

Pushka wants to solve this food puzzle. Can you solve it with him? All you need to do is follow the lines and find out the name of the vegetable.

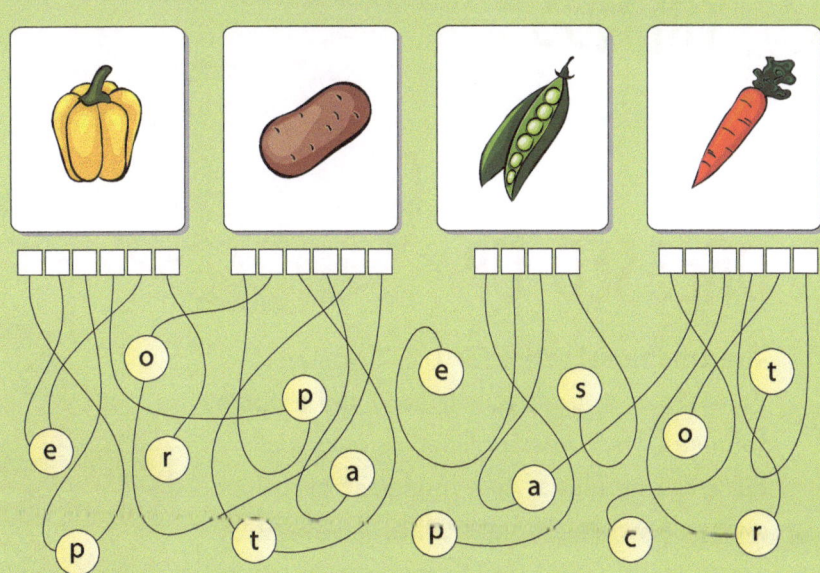

What to wear?

Daadu, there are so many tribes here, so the clothes people wear in this state must be unique!

Come along! Let's look at what the people of Chhattisgarh wear.

TRIBAL TRENDS

As we've seen, Chhattisgarh has been home to many tribes for centuries. The different tribes wear different styles of clothes, but all are imaginative and bright.

Tribal finery is very colourful. It's become popular as a fashion trend across the world.

DRESSED UP

The traditional attire for tribal women consists of a *lugda* (a half sari) and a *polkha* (blouse). They wear brilliant colours and different headgear too. In almost all tribes, women love wearing elaborate jewellery.

FANCY DURING FESTIVALS

During festivals, women become even more creative. They wear different ornaments, like bead necklaces, feathers in their hair and cowrie shells as jewellery.

MEN'S STYLE

Tribal men also love colour. In most tribes, like the Halbas and the Murias, men wear dhotis along with bright, cotton turbans. Sometimes turbans have an added accessory in the form of a feather or flower.

Can I also try on this headgear?

COSTUME
WORDGRID

This crossword has the names of some of the things the people of Chhattisgarh like to wear. Can you find them?

Q	B	X	C	V	B	N	M
F	E	A	T	H	E	R	S
S	A	Y	U	F	M	P	H
D	D	L	R	B	Q	S	E
G	S	K	B	V	W	K	L
H	J	A	A	C	D	I	L
J	E	A	N	S	T	R	S
G	J	K	O	I	U	T	L
G	D	H	O	T	I	G	H
H	F	L	O	W	E	R	S

Autograph, please?

There must be some super famous people in Chhattisgarh, right, Daadu?

Yes, that's for sure. Many famous people were born here, while some have made their home here. Let's meet a few of them.

TEEJAN BAI

She is a famous folk singer and artiste who performs the Pandavani style of singing. At one time, this was dominated by men. But she worked hard to make it acceptable for women too. She even won the Padma Shri for her contribution to this art.

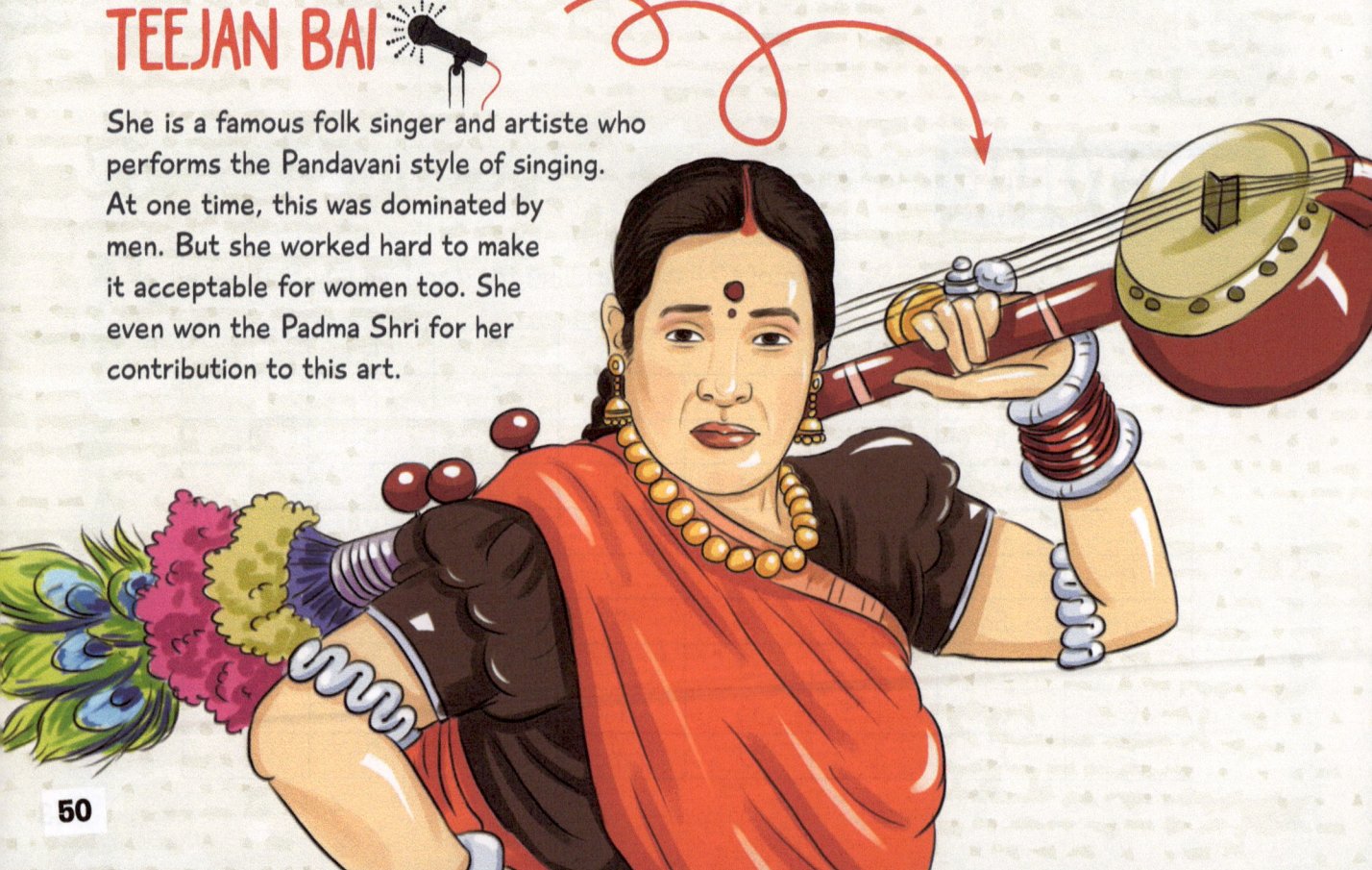

SATYADEV DUBEY

He was a famous director, actor and playwright, who has directed many famous plays in Hindi and English as well. He has also won many awards, like the Sangeet Natak Akademi Award and the Padma Bhushan too.

THAKUR PYARELAL SINGH

He was a famous freedom fighter who fought long and hard for India's freedom from the British. He was known as Tyaagmurti, meaning 'the epitome of sacrifice'.

HABIB TANVIR

He was a famous playwright, theatre director, actor and poet. He wrote many plays in Urdu and Hindi. He worked closely with several tribes and set up a theatre company called Naya Theater. He's written and directed some of India's most famous plays.

KUNWAR BAI YADAV

This spirited woman is said to have been more than a hundred years old; sadly, she passed away in February 2018. She lived in a tiny village in Chhattisgarh. Her home had no toilet for the longest time. Inspired by the government's Swachh Bharat campaign, she sold seven goats and built a toilet in her home. She became an example of forward thinking and was even visited by the prime minister of India.

So many famous people!

TRIAMBAK SHARMA

He is a famous cartoonist who founded one of India's few cartoon magazines, *Cartoon Watch*. He also established an educational institution to teach students the art of cartooning.

VINOD KUMAR SHUKLA

He is a famous modern Hindi writer who has written many novels. His style of writing is unique. Some of his novels have been adapted into movies too!

KRANTI TRIVEDI

She was a famous author who wrote wonderful novels in Hindi. Her work was so popular and read by so many that the government of India issued a stamp in her honour.

LESLIE CLAUDIUS

He was one of India's most successful hockey players. During his career, he won gold and silver Olympic medals. He was part of the Indian hockey team that had a winning streak in the 1950s and 1960s.

CELEBRITY MATCH

Match the name of the famous person, with what they are famous for.

| Leslie Claudius | Kranti Trivedi | Teejan Bai | Satyadev Dubey |

| Folk singer | Hockey player | Author | Playwright and director |

Once upon a time . . .

That was an interesting trip, Daadu. Now it's time for a story. Do you have one for us from this state?

Oh, yes, I do. You see, tribal folklore has been passed down from people to their children. The story I will tell you is a favourite of the Gond tribe. It's about Lord Rama and his brother Laxman, and you won't find it in the Ramayana.

LAXMAN AND THE FLUTE

Gond legend says that Lord Rama was also the king of the Gond kingdom. One day, Rama was angry with Laxman because of something he had done. As punishment, he did not allow Laxman to play his beloved flute.

Laxman simply loved playing the flute. He would lose himself in the music for hours and hours. Now he had been forbidden by his older brother, and he always obeyed him. But this time the call of the flute was too much to ignore.

When Laxman could bear it no more, he picked up his flute and began to play it. Soon he was lost in the music. He shut his eyes and played and played and played. The lilting music floated through the forest and reached the heavens.

Hearing this magical sound, an angel called Sonpari descended to Earth, following the haunting music. When she saw Laxman playing, she was enchanted.

But Laxman was too lost in his music to notice her. Sonpari felt insulted. She was not used to being ignored. She flung her glass bangles at Laxman. The glass broke into a thousand pieces and lay by Laxman's feet.

When Sita, Rama's wife, got back from the forests, where she had been collecting flowers, she saw the shards of glass on the ground.

'What have you done?' she exclaimed in horror. She thought Laxman had harmed some poor woman. When Rama saw this, he too was furious. He ordered Laxman to leave his kingdom and go away.

Laxman, obedient as ever, went off into the forest with his beloved flute. He wandered until he grew exhausted and decided to sit below a tree.

The Earth Goddess took pity on him. She appeared before Laxman. 'Follow that path and you will find a place where you will be welcomed,' she said.

Laxman followed her directions. Soon he found himself in a land that lay below this world. It was ruled by a king called Sheshnag. When the king met Laxman, he was smitten by his personality.

He got his only daughter married to Laxman. Laxman happily lived there for many years. But soon it was time to return to his real home.

I must go back home to my brother, he thought. He told his wife, whom he loved dearly, to be ready to leave the next day. But when King Sheshnag heard this, he stopped him.

'No, Laxman, my daughter cannot go to Earth with you,' he explained. 'She is from the land below Earth. We cannot survive up there. You must go alone.'

Laxman was devastated. He didn't want to leave his wife. But he couldn't stay with her either.

When it was time to leave, Sheshnag gave him a farewell gift. It was a trunk full of diamonds.

'Take this. But remember, do not open it till you get home. Else you will repent,' he warned Laxman.

Laxman accepted it with a heavy heart. He left to go on the long journey home.

On the way, he wondered why the box was so heavy. He remembered Sheshnag's warning, but his curiosity overtook him. He put the trunk down and opened it. To his amazement, his beloved wife was in the trunk.

'Why did you open the lid?' she moaned. 'Now I will have to leave you forever.' Saying this, she disappeared into the sky with a clap of thunder.

Poor Laxman was left full of regret and grief. He called out to his wife again and again, but all he heard was the sound of crashing thunder.

To this day, the people of the Gond tribe believe that when it thunders, it is actually Laxman calling out to his adored wife.

TRAVEL DIARY

Have you enjoyed this trip to Chhattisgarh with your friends Mishki and Pushka—and, of course, with Daadu Dolma?

Now you can make your own Chhattisgarh diary. And if you ever visit Chhattisgarh, make sure you take pictures and put them in the photo box.

The first place I would visit in Chhattisgarh:

_____

I think the most interesting historical figure from Chhattisgarh is:

_____

The one dish I am definitely going to eat:

_____

The monument I think is the most interesting:

_____

The one famous person from Chhattisgarh I would love to meet:

_____

If I were from Chhattisgarh, I would learn this dance:

_____

The festival from Chhattisgarh that I think is the most fun:

_____

The five words that I think describe Chhattisgarh the best are:

_____

_____

_____

_____

_____

My Chhattisgarh memories:

ANSWERS

page 9 RANGE TRICK

SNOWY, SLOPE, PEAK, STEEP

page 11 NATURE WORD SEARCH

D	F	D	T	E	A	K	B	V	B	A
T	I	G	E	R	Y	U	H	E	R	Q
Q	W	E	R	G	G	H	A	S	I	W
S	D	S	A	L	A	I	X	Z	K	E
B	L	A	C	K	B	U	C	K	J	R
Z	M	N	B	V	C	S	A	L	Y	T
F	H	T	V	W	Q	J	A	B	H	G
S	P	O	T	T	E	D	D	E	E	R
X	F	H	Y	E	N	A	D	E	W	Q
Z	B	A	M	B	O	O	C	F	G	J
X	C	V	H	M	Z	X	C	N	K	X
Z	T	N	W	E	O	O	P	Z	X	V

page 13 WHAT'S ODD?

VILLAGE, BULLOCK CART, HUT

page 17 SAME OR DIFFERENT

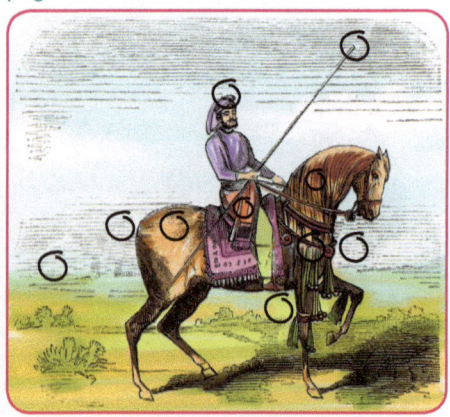

page 21 MATCH THE WORDS

What?—Ka?; Where did you come from?—Tain kati le aaye has?; Yes, of course—Haaho; You—Tain; Your—Tor; What is your name?—Tor naam kaa haawaye?

page 23 WORD JUMBLE

GOND, BHATRA, MURIA, HALBA, KOL, MUNDA

page 25 SING SONG

play, know, pool, shops

page 27 DANCE DELIGHT

Waltz, Samba, Kathakali, Ballet, Garba, Bharatanatyam, Dandiya Raas, Bhangra, Cha cha cha, Jive

page 29 SHADOW MATCH

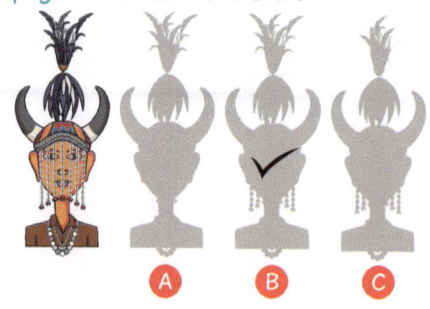

A   B   C

page 37 CAVE MAZE

The rope in Pushka's hand will get them out.

page 38-39 MONUMENT SPOTTING

page 41 HIDDEN WORDS

Here are some of the words you can form: aid, aim, air, and, ash, day, dam, bun, him, his, man, may, nail, busy, dial, dual, dumb, land, hair, yard

page 47 FOOD PUZZLE

Pepper, Potato, Peas, Carrot

page 49 COSTUME WORDGRID

Q	B	X	C	V	B	N	M
F	E	A	T	H	E	R	S
S	A	Y	U	F	M	P	H
D	D	L	R	B	Q	S	E
G	S	K	B	V	W	K	L
H	J	A	A	C	D	I	L
J	E	A	N	S	T	R	S
G	J	K	O	I	U	T	L
G	D	H	O	T	I	G	H
H	F	L	O	W	E	R	S

page 53 CELEBRITY MATCH

Leslie Claudius—Hockey player; Kranti Trivedi—Author; Teejan Bai—Folk singer; Satyadev Dubey—Playwright and director